OTHER BOOKS BY GEORGIA S. MCDADE

Travel Tips for Dream Trips

Outside the Cave 1

Outside the Cave 2

Outside the Cave 3

Outside the Cave 4

Observations and Revelations

OUTSIDE THE CAVE

4

GEORGIA S. McDADE

Outside the Cave 4 © 2016, 2019 Georgia S. McDade

All rights reserved. No part of this publication may be reproduced or transmitted in any form or by any means, electronic or mechanical, including photocopy, recording, or any information storage and retrieval system now known or to be invented, without permission in writing of the author, except by reviewers who wish to quote brief passages in connection with a review written for publication in print and electronic form.

Cover Art © Adam Korpak

Book & Cover Design by Vladimir Verano, Vertvolta design
www.vertvoltapress.com

Contact the author:

gsmcdade@msn.com

FIRST EDITION

ISBN: 978-0-9821872-3-4

To Peggy McIntosh, author of
"Unpacking the Invisible Knapsack of White Privilege"

Tim Wise author of *White Like Me: Reflections on Race from a Privileged Son*

Jim Wallis, author of
America's Original Sin: Racism, White Privilege, and the Bridge to a New America

These three persons have been instrumental in informing millions of whites in America and elsewhere about the race problem and how to solve the race problem. Naming the problem, admitting their part in the problem, and attempting to rectify the problem are great contributions toward the solution. Though the end is nowhere near, we have progressed as much as we have because of the understanding of these persons and the steady protest of persons who have fought and do fight, as Lisa Sharon Harper says, "colonization, imperialism, slavery, patriarchy, exploitation, and ecological consumption."

To all of the participants—past, present, and future—in the battle to solve the problem

To the many persons who have read and shared the poetry, thanked me, and encouraged me to continue—I thank you.

So many truths seem to be rushing at me as the result of things felt and seen and lived through. Oh what I think I must tell this world! Oh the time that I crave—and the peace—and the power!

~ Lorraine Hansberry, *To Be Young, Gifted, and Black*

"A poet's work: to name the unnameable, to point at frauds, to take sides, start arguments, shape the world, and stop it going to sleep."

~Salman Rushdie

ACKNOWLEDGEMENTS

Minnie Collins for writing the foreword.

All of the Gallery 110 artists whose work always inspired and often taught me.

All of the readers, especially the ones who commented.

Georgia S. McDade, Ph. D.

CONTENTS

(Poems listed in the order they appear in the book.)

Foreword   i

INTERROGATIVES

    Where Is God?   1
    What Is God Doing?   2
    Questions   3
    Arguments Against the Death Penalty   5
    Muscle and Might   6
    Fragility   8
    To the Lady Who Wanted to Know
        What Kind of Messiah Could Not
        Get the Job Done the First Time   9
    The List Goes On   10
    Halloween Horror   11
    Sanctioned Murder   13
    Titanic Errors   14
    No Boundaries   15

EXCLAMATIONS

    Culture   19
    This Is Going On   20
    That Don't Take No Sense   22
    The Simple Things   23
    The Interview   24
    Images of Crying Women   25
    An Act   27
    Who's Lying   28
    Living in the Present   29

Surprised Again	30
Youth or the Sea?	31
Adam and Eve and That Fruit	33
I Thought Wrong	34
The Problem with the Minimum	36
The Real Spectrum	37
Don't Call Me Mother!	38
The Greens	40
Two Lovely Couples	41
Dali Clocks	43

Imperatives

Journals Never Written	47
The 545: Those Who Hold the Reins	48
Past Time	50
Projection	51
Laces	51
A Time Not to Ignore…	52
Funerals	54
A Spring Chorus	55
Take Pictures!	56
No, They Can't!	57

Declarations

Life Lesson	61
Inside and Outside the Cave	61
Protection Nullified	62
What We Are	63
A Young Malawian …	64
A Picture	65
Irrelevancies	67
Brain Dead	68
Excuses	69
Folly of Agreeing to Disagree	70

The Ambivalence of Sharing	72
Worse Than Infidelity	73
One-Sided Slights	74
You Know That You Know	75
A Terrible Sadness	76
Deceptive Looks	77
Every Student Can Learn	78
Doing and Being	79
Crumbling	80
Present: After 50 Years	81
Post-Traumatic-Stress Syndrome	82
Responses	83
A Warning	84
Carrying the Ball	85
My Undone List	89
High School Reunions	90
A Man Worth Admiring	91
The Ignorant Prodigal	93
If You Lived Here	94
What You're Getting Into	96
Relativity	97
The Message	97

Musings

Plusses and Minuses	101
What Is Sanity?	101
Questions That Don't Need to Be Asked	102
What Folks Miss	102
That Shakespeare Mind	103
Wondering and Knowing	105
My Mom's Letters	106
What to Keep	107
Christian: The Lion	108
Duped	110
Unmarried	111

Starting Again	112
In the Same Situations	113
What Would You Do?	114
The Sound of Children	115
The Cracked Window	116
Index	123
About the Author	129

Foreword

"Poets write because they must; because they have an inner drive."
~Dudley Randall, African-American poet (1914-2000)

WRITING STORIES SINCE SHE WAS EIGHT YEARS OLD, Dr. Georgia S. McDade is a poet, journalist, short story writer, and world traveler. Her fourth book in the *Outside the Cave* series is a collection of ninety-one poems in which she probes myriad hypocritical attitudes. preconceptions, fears, and frustrations tempered with hope. *Outside the Cave IV* has four sections: Interrogatives, Exclamations, Imperatives, and Declarations. Using an ironic somewhat sarcastic tenor, she peppers her poems with folksy syntax in " That Don't Make No Sense" and "Mama" as well as with classical allusions to Shakespeare's characters.

The first section, "Interrogatives," is a whirlwind of humiliation, powerlessness, and angst trapped in a storm of unanswered questions. McDade's litany of "wants" in "God's Doings" and "What Is God Doing?" questions the fragility of life, the death penalty, and the voracious humiliation of Black lives.

As a reprieve to these political oppressions, she seeks balance in "Exclamations," the second section. Here she yearns for the "Simple Things" and knows the "real spectrum" of life includes positives such as joy, love, nature, hope, family pictures and negatives such as unfairness, sadness, disappointment, lies, hate, meanness, and death. While questioning cultural traditions, she uncovers the irony of misappropriated funds for minor rather than major needs for the future in "This Is Going On." Yet youth, knowing their historical memories, can design a different future where they can stand up and declare, "I got this!" in "Youth or the Sea."

Holding on to memories is essential to "Imperatives," the third section. In "Journals Never Written," she yearns for her mother's letters, never kept, never written in a journal, or too soon forgotten. With an inner longing, she wants to write about compassionate moments with her mother. Her disappointment continues in "The 545: Those Who Hold The Reins" where she reveals that 545 people in the United States interpret and decide the validity and fulfillment of the American Constitution.

In the last and longest section of forty-nine poems, "Declarations" opens with "Life Lessons" followed by "Inside and Outside of the Cave," a part of the book's title. Again visceral discomfort hovers in poems about infidelity, sanity, anxiety, powerlessness, disappointment, and—perhaps—some hope. Power permeates her relations with a government whose "Protection [is] Nullified." Hope rather than despair, however, hovers over the conversations between a "Malawian Male and American Female Talk Dreams and Change." Both muse that change happens first in self–examination and sharing knowledge. Yet, Dr. McDade continues to question our sagacity to change or begin sincere conversations.

Outside the Cave IV, filled with insightful poems and rich syntax, might benefit from a different arrangement and grouping of poems. Nevertheless, a primary strength in *Outside the Cave IV* is its gamut of complexities which must be unraveled in order for us to have an inner drive to question, alter, and change tattered social, political, and economic constructs.

Minnie A. Collins, English Faculty Emeritus, Seattle Central College
April 16, 2016

INTERROGATIVES

Where Is God?

A woman asked Dear Abby, "Where was God when my son was being brutally killed?"

Abby responded, "The same place He was when His Son was being brutally killed."

"Good answer," said I, "but not satisfactory."

I see God everywhere—the greenery, mountains, sunshine, moonlight, lakes and oceans, newborn babies, happy children—and I am grateful.

Still I want.

I want the wars stopped.

I want immigrants home where most would rather be and welcomed wherever they are or have to be.

I want the homeless housed.

I want the sick healed.

I want the hungry fed.

I want the innocent freed.

I want the "poorly educated" educated.

So, I ask, "Where is God?"

I know God sees everything I've mentioned.

I know God knows everything I've mentioned.

I know God could solve every problem.

And yet, so many problems, especially big ones are not solved.

I'm missing something.

I end where the mother began: Where is God?

1/21/16

What Is God Doing?

What is God doing?
Wars are everywhere.
Immigrants are daily made.
The hungry and homeless roam the streets.
Sick people go without care, die early for lack of care.

Surely God does not expect us puny people to eliminate these problems.
And then an explosive answer rings out: "We people created these problems."
Maybe the question isn't what is God doing but rather what are we doing.
Perhaps God does indeed expect us to solve the problems!

1/21/16

Questions

All of my questions are not for God.

I have lots of questions for my fellowman.

I would like to know if James Earl Ray believed he could kill
    the dream by killing the dreamer.

I would like to know if Mark David Chapman is satisfied that he
    killed John Lennon.

I would like to know if Sirhan Sirhan believes killing RFK was a
    good deed.

I would like to know if any of the legions who killed blacks
    and whites during the Civil Rights Movement believe they did the right
    thing and, if so, why.

I would like to know if all of those demonstrators who protested the enrollment
    of little black boys and girls entering schools believe they did the right
    thing. (I know Hazel at Central High regrets her actions, says a
    person's life should not be branded by one action. But then I never saw
    where she hates she did it. She hates being recognized for having done
    it.)

I would like to know if Susan Smith still believes drowning
    her children was worth her dream of having her "boyfriend" in her life.

I would like to know if David M. Rice ever thinks
    about the Goldmark family and realizes how wrong he was.

I would like to know if Dr. Conrad Murray believes giving a
    patient what he/she wants, despite guidelines to the contrary, is ever
    permissible regardless of the doctor's pay.

I would like one or two of the mass murderers—Hitler, Pol Pot, Genghis
    Khan—to explain why they consider what they did acceptable.

I would like to know if medical professionals who conducted the
>	syphilis experiments over forty years on unsuspecting
>		individuals ever regretted how they changed lives.

Now you may wish to ask me why I want to know. Because these questions and others cross my mind, I tell myself that proper answers might make me forget. All of these acts are appalling to me; I would never have dreamed of committing any of them. I don't think the overwhelming majority of people in the world would think of committing and certainly not commit such deeds.

I would like to know what in the mind of an individual makes a fellow human
>	being think such acts solve problems or are condoned.

I would like to know if, prior to acting, they ever thought of any consequences
>	of their actions.

I would like to know if they think about their actions.

I would just like to know.

01/23/16

Arguments Against the Death Penalty

10 years, 20 years, 30 years, Life

One day is too long an incarceration for the innocent person.

Yet innocent people are relegated to prison, some to death sentences, others to death.

The preponderance of exonerations, especially since the advent of DNA tests, should halt death penalties.

Here are other reasons:

        Perjured testimony

        Inadequate defense

        Confused witness(es)

        Flawed investigations

        Inherent prejudice

        Official misconduct

        Misinterpreted evidence

        Mistaken evidence

        Invalid evidence

        Circumstantial evidence

        Misleading Evidence

What more proof is necessary?

02/04/15

Muscle and Might

America's Finest

The Blues

The Boys in Blue

Police

Powerful police

(Is there such a creature as powerless police? Yet citizens and
 courts are repeatedly asked not to "tie the hands of the
 police.")

Badges

Billy clubs

Spray

Tasers

Spikes

Shields

Grenades

Guns

And thanks to our military, add bayonets, armored tracked
 vehicles, grenade launchers, and high caliber firearms.

Today's police forces are armed better!

(Is there such a state as armed worse?)

Special **W**eapons **a**nd **T**actics (**SWAT**) teams are always ready with their
 carbines, sniper rifles, submachine guns, shotguns....

High-risk situations, especially those involving the mentally ill
 and young men of color, take precedence.

Might never was necessarily right.

This is still true.

Police will do their jobs.

Some of them will be injured, killed.

But generally, some of us can count on them inflicting more damage than they suffer.

Their power has been used, misused, and abused.

Still, police have the power.

Police are the power.

Maybe one day we the people will have that muscle, that power—and use it for good.

Maybe, just maybe, the might of the people will indeed make right?

05/09/15

Fragility

How fragile are we?
We don't know!
How can we possibly know?
The best we can do is speculate.
And the speculation may be off, extremely off.
What may drive one person over a cliff may propel another to the
    summit.
The time: one day we can take all heaped at and
    on us and not flinch; the next day the least problem breaks us.
How many times has someone killed him or herself after being the
    butt of a prank?
This person is not around when the prankster says, "I was just
    playing." Or I wanted to teach her/him a lesson; I never expected
    him/her to _____.
Or how many times has someone become a recluse, bully,
    rapist, or murderer after he or she has been injured?
Because we do not know the fragility score of an individual, we
    should err on the side of kindness rather than meanness.
Shouldn't we?

12/07/12

To the Lady Who Wanted to Know What Kind of Messiah Could Not Get the Job Done the First Time

"What kind of messiah could not get the job done the first time?" the Jewish
      teacher of the conversion class asked as a second thought
      after declaring the Messiah had not come.
"What kind of Messiah needs a Second Coming?"
Her question caught me off guard; I had never heard that question.
I was the only one stunned.
Everyone else had accepted the doctrine.
I was the only one present for academic reasons.
It's taken a long while, but perhaps here's a satisfactory answer:
The Messiah Who comes the second time is not One Who could
      not get the job done the first time.
This Messiah is the kind Who loves and cares, the kind Who forgives
      repeatedly, the kind Who provides opportunities even when we have
      squandered other opportunities.
All religions say Jesus was a good Person, a good role model.
Why a Second Coming?
Maybe this Messiah, being both human and divine, wanted to give us a second
      chance.
If you believe the Messiah exists, is coming, why not believe the Divine is
      giving us humans a second chance or more chances when we need
      them?

01/18/13

The List Goes On

Emmett

Freddie

Amadou

Trayvon

Eric

Mike

Ezell

Tamir

Add your memories.

The list goes on.
Soweto

Sudan

Rwanda

Watts

Baltimore

Add your cities and countries.
The list goes on.

There's a madness in the air.
But Hope is not dead.
Hope is fighting a horrendous battle with Ignorance.
And too many days it looks as if Ignorance is winning.
But Ignorance is not winning.
Right?

05/09/15

Halloween Horror

Tall, dark, and handsome.
An apt description if ever there was one.
Add friendly.
A beautiful smile, a warm greeting whenever I passed him on
    the street.
A good specimen of a human being, on every count I knew.
Add bold.
Had a party to raise funds to make the move from Seattle to L. A.
    so he could have more opportunities....
If you knew him, you probably made a contribution.
All he needed was access.
He was an actor extraordinaire.
ER, NYPD, Liar, Liar: who knows where he may have gone?

A neighbor complained to police about noise at the
    Halloween costume party.
The policeman reported, "fearful for my safety and my
    life," he shot actor Anthony Lee.
The coroner reported Lee was shot "once in the back of the
    head and three times in the back."
The uncostumed target pointing the toy gun died at the scene.
Nine rounds of ammunition fired.
Justifiable homicide.

No one knows when the imposing thirty-nine-year-old actor
> first said, "I'm the perfect target; I'll probably be killed by the police."

All of us survivors know he was right.

He died at the scene, never knowing his prediction was right on.

Remembering Anthony Lee
Killed October 29, 2000, in Los Angeles *05/10/15*

Sanctioned Murder

How many innocent persons has the state killed?
No one knows but God.
And, once again, He is not telling.

We now know the Rosenbergs, especially Ethel, should not have been killed;
 she was innocent.
How many groups are exonerating the incarcerated as often as time and money
 allow?
How many other innocent persons have been killed?
Some argue the guilty—often poor and not white—should not be killed.
The state is doing what it is punishing a person for doing!
The state, of course, can do what the individual can't!
But we—most of us—think the state ought to build rather than destroy.
How many other persons should the state have not killed?
For the US to have killed fewer persons than China, Iran, and Saudi
 Arabia in the number of persons killed in one year is good.
Better would be not to be on the list!

01/23/16

Titanic Errors

In no particular order, here are some of the errors that contributed to the sinking of the *Titanic*:
Human error/Pilot error
Rudeness
Pettiness
Direct hit as opposed to side hit
Low quality wrought iron
Women and children first as opposed to women and children only
Partially full lifeboats
Excessive speed in iceberg water
Insufficient number of lifeboats
Out-of-date safety regulations
Design of ship
Chain of events
Direction, height of bulkheads
Switched off wireless (radio)
Distance iceberg traveled
Key to case with binoculars in it accidentally taken from Titanic
Missed messages
A few more reasons probably could be added.
How many errors could have been corrected?
Is there one person responsible—for the crash? Warning? Exit?
Selfishness isn't on the list?
Greed?
Arrogance cannot be on the list?
I wish those travelers could see and sail on today's Titanics.
(I also wish car manufacturers would take heed.)

01/23/16

No Boundaries

Condoms pricked
Semen stolen
Lies about performed vasectomies and unused birth control
Children conceived for the wrong reasons,
Unwanted by one parent, sometimes neither

Wars—begun on false evidence and prolonged on equally
       false evidence
Lives inevitably lost
Is there nothing sacred?
No lines in the sand?
No parameters, boundaries?
Stop signs?
Do-not-go signs?
Scruples?
Morals?
Cheaters are all around us, always manipulating us, changing history in little
       ways and big ways, unwilling to let the unfolding proceed
       naturally, damning not only us the living but them the unborn.
How could they?

01/12/14

EXCLAMATIONS

Culture

Culture calls for male circumcision.
Culture calls for female circumcision.
Culture calls for female feet binding.
Culture calls for slavery.
Culture calls for scarring.
There's no telling what else Culture requires.

Culture can annihilate us all?
Just give it time.

01/21/16

This Is Going On

Move generators from basements.
Automated tellers return charge cards immediately.
Call patients to remind them of appointments.
Locate freezers at bottom of refrigerators.
Motorize wheelchairs.
Manufacture wheeled luggage for everyone.
Add lifts to buses.
Affix bike carriers to buses.
Flatten curbs for wheeled vehicles.
Improve cars with rearview cameras, blind spot lights,
    automatic windshield wipers, permanently attached gas caps, etc.
Transplant hearts, lungs, kidneys.

All of the above and many more improvements are minor when we can or don't
    do anything about the major changes below:
Failing crops
Decreasing crop yields
Dying coral reefs
Melting glaciers and ice caps
Collapsing sea ice
Decreasing wetlands
Rising sea level
Intensifying heat waves
 Heavy rain
Acidifying oceans
Diminishing water supplies
Migrating fish and other water creatures toward the Poles

Species becoming extinct…

Global warming
Climate changing
Temperature rising

What other signs do we need?
Do they believe Earth can take care of itself?
Perhaps Marvin Gaye could have made them see!

01/23/16 (begun in 2014)

That Don't Make No Sense!

M'Dear was a stickler for using good English.
Yet there were times when something happened, and she would blurt, "That
    don't make no sense!"
When I see a person can kill
    for sneakers, a cell phone, a car;
    because music is too loud or a car alarm won't shut off;
    because certain persons were in *his* neighborhood;
    his children and the woman who bore them;
    her children to keep her "boyfriend."
I find myself thinking, "That don't make no sense."

03/18/14

The Simple Things

Sun and rain
Sky and sea
Sand and dirt
Simple things
We wondered not about their origins.
We simply savored their presence.

Simple things of another breed
Grass and flowers
We wallowed in the one and carefully picked the other, usually for Mother.
Storms and clouds produced no fear—
      or fear easily assuaged by Mom and Dad.
We knew not trouble.
Oh, the joy, the peace of those days!
A natural high if ever there was one!
And like many American kids everywhere, we had no idea how good simple is.

08/12/06   Inspired by Liz Tran paintings

The Interview

I saw your watery eyes.

I saw how you attempted to hold back the tears.

I thought you did not want me to see.

I tried not to see.

I don't want anyone to see, know frustration can make me cry.

I thought perhaps you felt the same.

I did nothing because I did not know what to do.

I had never seen anyone cry for me, my situation.

I wanted to cry for your tears.

I could not see how crying would help.

I really wanted neither of us to cry.

I admit tears come as I try to capture the brief time.

We had a job to do!

Two women—one Japanese, one Black, both Americans in the only home they know—sharing their separate pain, yet realizing someone of a different heritage understood.

So slavery was worse; internment was neither camp nor vacation.

Descendants continue, not always preoccupied with the injustice but occasionally sharing a story, a repercussion of the inequality that in various ways makes all Americans smaller.

02/11/16

Images of Crying Women

Images of crying women abound in media and in my head.
There are days when I think the images will never stop
    coming; they know no order nor impact.
Little naked Phan Thi Kim Phuc running in Vietnam
(But then they tell me all is fair in love and war.)
Little older fourteen-year-old runaway Mary Ann Vecchio at Kent
    State
The still older, stoic Mrs. JFK, no visible tears from her: we know enough
    about her life to know there were many tears, silent tears.
Mrs. Medgar Evers
Mrs. Malcolm X
Mrs. MLK
Mrs. RFK and that momentary face of fear on Mrs. JFK at RFK's funeral….
Mothers of violently killed children, incurably ill children
And the list goes on.
Apparently no one can say what's going on.
Certainly no one seems to be able to stop what's going on!
Add all of those unknown girls and women, immediate caregivers
    of or gravediggers for daddies and brothers and uncles and
        husbands, fiancés, cousins, and friends….and now mothers, sisters, and
        aunts, wives, fiancées.
Add all of those victims of wars declared and not, those wars by
    any other names, those actions that leave persons as dead
    as war does.
Add drone casualties, especially those whom we did not intend
    to kill, those for whose lives we apologize, collateral damage
    McVeigh taught me.

Apparently someone thinks an accidental death is less painful
    than an intended death.
And don't forget those who deserved our wrath.
Remember the victims of terrorism.
Remember those Marys of centuries ago, especially that one
    depicted in *The Pieta* of the gentle Michelangelo.
Life and literature, the images are there: those Lysistrata women
    who took matters into their hands, the guilty Mrs.
    Hutchinson
And the images keep coming via violence, racism, greed,
    accidents….
Nature adds to the list indiscriminately with her tsunamis and
    earthquakes, wildfires, volcanoes, and floods.
Images won't go away.
Still some of us wonder if some day soon we'll cease our
    seething and see the last image of a crying woman.
And from I know not where yet clearly I know this: not soon will we
    see the last image of a crying woman.

07/18/13

An Act

A grope
Sex
Traffic
Bribery
Embezzling
Photo

They confessed, or someone revealed.
They suffer; sometimes others suffer more.
One act could've been avoided.
Now someone—or more than one—pays and pays
      because of this one act that can't be undone.

01/11/14

Who's Lying?

She finally caught up with him.
Said she wanted to know why he lied.
(The wise among us are grateful to discover the lie; the why of
      the lie does not change the lie!)
How was he to know he couldn't, wouldn't keep his word?
He meant every word when he said it; he said he did!
Sometimes he was responsible; other times he was irresponsible.
And this she knew, knew well.
But things happened, not without cause.
Things happened in the midst of causes over which perhaps he had little or no
      control.
He was sorry she was hurt.
But, he reasoned, that was something else he could not control.
And he was sorry he had to run; he had another engagement.

01/04/14

Living in the Present

One day at a time.
How I wish I could do one day at a time!
Just one more admonition that needs qualifying!
I would love to do one day at a time.
But the past and the future double-team me.
Something from yesterday spills into today.
Something from today spills into tomorrow.

Well-meaning folks advise us to live in the present.
We do!
We can live only in the present.
The implication in one day at a time is that past, present, and future are not connected.
But they are!
They are intertwined, regardless of how we attempt to separate them.
Consider background.
Consider medical care.
Consider education.
Consider a career.
Consider a mate.
Consider support.
Consider. Consider!
Actions in the past often control the future.
Failure to act or act properly, wisely in the present affects the future.
So often we act as we do because of some plus or minus in the past.
We are what we are or aren't because of the past!
What we are or aren't in the present affects the future!
Please, no more reminders to live in the present.

11/07/13

"I must study politics and war, that my sons may have the liberty to study mathematics and philosophy, natural history and naval architecture, in order to give their children a right to study painting, poetry, music, architecture, tapestry, and porcelain."

~John Adams
2nd President of the United States

Surprised Again

John Adams maintained he had to "study politics and war so that
    his SONS"—he excluded his one surviving daughter—would have
    the liberty to study mathematics and philosophy, natural
    history and naval architecture" and his grandchildren would
    have the "right to study painting, poetry, music, architecture,
    tapestry, and porcelain."
I am baffled that it did not occur to him that other parents may
    have wanted the same for their sons and daughters.
I am baffled that he never saw slave parents and thought they
    might have wanted the same for their children.

12/04/14

Youth or the Sea?

Old Marlowe wondered if the excitement, the joy he felt at sea stemmed from the sea or youth.

I got this!
There's no need to wonder!
It was youth!
A journalist gathering news
A Peace Corps volunteer amazing a child
A teacher seeing the growth of a mind
A detective fighting crime
A politician stamping out evil
A cowboy roping a steer
Anyone winning the sport race

All of the above plus many more!
It's youth!
That time of trust—in others and ourselves
That time of belief—in others and ourselves
That time of invincibility, spontaneity, impulse, risk-taking
That time we work to change the world
That time we know we can change the world
That time, that time
No mortgages, no taxes, no ill health—no thought of any headaches of any kind.
Youth, that's the time!

Granted, everyone is not so fortunate to have such a youth.
But those who had it know it.
They never thought about it while they were in it.
Marlowe was asking a rhetorical question.
He knew all along the sea was simply the setting.
The feeling stems from youth.

Inspired by British writer Joseph Conrad's short story "Youth" and Australian writer Geoffrey Bewley who believed he was Conrad's reincarnation   *01/28/16*

Adam and Eve and That Fruit

If God had told Adam and Eve the repercussions of
        eating the fruit, perhaps they would not have eaten it.
Because God knows everything, created the Tree of
        Knowledge AND Adam and Eve, He had to know
        they would eat the fruit.
He had to know that the best way to get some of us to do
        something is tell us not to do it.
He had to know.

Fair, I guess, does not enter the picture.
And if wishes were horses....
Anyway, I wish they had not eaten that fruit.
Repercussions and repercussions of repercussions still abound.

Some days, I can't help wishing they had not eaten that fruit.

08/19/15

I Thought Wrong

I think I could have done it!
I do.
I think if I'd been Eve, I would not have let the serpent
      convince me to eat the fruit.
I think if I'd been Adam, I would not have let Eve
      convince me to taste the fruit.
I think about all the times I followed the rules.
Sometimes I hated the rules, but I reasoned that the
      persons before me had endured certain experiences
      and came to certain conclusions, and, therefore, the
      rules were for my own good.
That's what I reasoned.
Rarely can I think of a time I broke the rule, colored
      outside the lines, got outside of the box.
But I admit there were times; I had to find another
      way, had to color outside the lines, or get outside the
      box.
 I did not always follow the "normal" path; some
      situations demanded that I break the rule, upset
      the norm.
Here's a time:
I drank from the white fountain, a punishable offense
      said the law.
But I did!
I was only eight, did not confess until I was out of the
      city, among friends, seventeen.

Only then did I learn that each of the seven or eight of
       us girls in the college dormitory had broken the
       law though we were in different places at the time!
But this was the law all over Louisiana.
And all of us had drunk from the white fountain!
Wow, I guess I might have eaten that fruit!

08/19/15

The Problem with the Minimum

"I did the minimum."
"What," said she?
"I did the minimum," said the man.
"But why would you do the minimum?"
"I just do the minimum."
Another first for her, a sentence she had never spoken, heard:
> "I do the minimum."

Tape, glue, Velcro, a safety pin, nail polish—the
> minimum for the minute, of course, usually ok.

But properly repair for the long haul; the optimal is needed.
A person could get hurt!
People could die!
This is information worth knowing.
So much now makes sense.
Attention: people everywhere need to know there are
> folk out there, charging, charging a high price for the minimum.

Folks need to know when they're getting the minimum.
Now, if all of the minimum folk would confess, we could
> get a world really going.

01/10/16

The Real Spectrum

In an instant
Eat a dinner
See a play
Hear a band
Watch a game

People being people
People enjoying life

Simultaneously,

Other people being people
People destroying life

Spoil the dinner
Stop the play
Stifle the band
Suspend the game
      How broad the spectrum among *homo sapiens*!

11/14/15

Don't Call Me Mother!

The first time someone called me "M'am?" I replied, "M'am is
 what they call my mom."
For a while after that reply, I appeared to accept m'am but
 cringed a bit inside whenever I heard it.
I do not recall when I stopped responding, began taking it in
 stride though occasionally I still wanted to say, "M'am is
 what they call my mom."
Then one day, grayer admittedly, something happened to
 remind me of that first "m'am."
A Black female cashier at Penney's last year called me
 "mother."
Thrice in 2013 I've been called "mother" or "mama":
By a male Hispanic duct cleaner in my home
By a black male clerk at the supermarket
By an Asian waitress at a restaurant.
I didn't know these persons!
I'd never seen these persons!
I don't doubt their sincerity, their desire to show me respect.
And I do believe they were showing me respect.
The one person I told about this feeling said the same: calling you
 mother is a sign of respect.
I'm not ready for their signs of respect!
And I mean no disrespect to them.
I have no children.
I AM NOT THEIR MOTHER!
Respect someone else.
Respect me differently.
Perhaps in twenty years I'll be more accepting.

Perhaps.
And then I remembered, I've lived seventeen years longer than my mom lived.
I'll probably continue to cringe at being called mom or mother.
I'll probably never like it, but I can smile; I won't get upset.
Presently, "Good Morning," "Good Afternoon," or "Good
      Evening" works fine!

10/25/13

And then in 2016 I went to Malawi.
Lo and behold, everyone called me "Mother!"
The immigration official in Zambia called me mother!
Until I color my hair, I will no longer protest.
I will accept their mode of respect.

01/21/16

The Greens

New growth green!
Old growth green!

Fern
Oak
Spruce
Elm
Alder
Pine
Crayola can't touch this!

04/16/15

Two Lovely Couples

Two men, loved two women dearly
Wedded their choice
Certain they knew where they were headed
Whom they married.
Two women, loved two men dearly
Wedded their choice
Certain they knew where they were headed
 Whom they married.

A few years passed.
And then Reality set in!
Something whispered all is not well in his and then her ear.
The whispering was not the same, nor at the same time.
But the whisper grew louder.
The two in each couple had different ideas about where they were headed,
Exceedingly different ideas they eventually realized!
How did they ever get together?
Well, somehow, maybe, perhaps—they never got to the core
        issues.
Maybe the cores changed, or one's core changed.

Whatever, each one now treads a separate path, alternately blaming self or the
        other, alternately wondering how could he/she have been so wrong, so
        stupid, so gullible.
Maybe one day someone can make them see or they themselves will realize
        what a miracle is taking place when two persons successfully and
        honestly make a life together.

Maybe they will see neither the ingredients nor the amounts for a happy marriage are spelled out. They make the recipe as they go—together—always listening, respecting, sharing, caring, and, of course, loving.

01/23/16

Dali Clocks

I love the Dali clocks!
But I can't look at them daily!
They're usually wrong.
The two times a day when they are right, I am long gone.
The clocks remind me to ignore Time or do a better job of pretending I ignore Time.
Regular clocks are either too slow or too fast.
BUT THEY STEADILY TICK!
They always remind me that I am a slave of Time.
They remind me that I have to gather records or record at gatherings.
They remind me there is rarely one thing, but usually several things to do plus something else, OFTEN UNPLANNED AND UNDESIRED!
They always remind me of a date, a meeting, a program, a DEADLINE.
So many tasks scream to be done!
Responsible me seems always not only to hear the scream but answer.
I must work the works of Him and others.
But in Daliland I get a break!

05/30/10

IMPERATIVES

Journals Never Written

I wish I had kept my teen-age journals rather than leaving them at
        home where someone threw them away.

I wish I had kept a journal of the six-week National Science
        Foundation Summer Program for High-Ability Students.

I wish I had a journal of the years of getting a doctorate. I was
        slow to see the racism. Maybe I could understand now.

I wish I had a journal of the team-taught classes at Seattle Central.
There was that class Sex in the Gay Nineties: faculty and students
        had different definitions of "gay."

I wish I had a journal of the two years I taught at Lakeside. One of
        the fellow teachers said, "Lakeside shook your tree." It took
        a while for me to understand what she meant and agree she
        was right. But I too shook some trees.

I wish I had a journal of all of those trips to the Oregon
        Shakespeare Festival, beginning in 1971.

Sometimes it is nice to compare then and now, see what I said, felt.
Sometimes writing from my past explains my present self to me.
Sometimes a good analysis is helpful.

So, keep a journal.
You can always destroy what you don't want.
But you can never examine what you never wrote.

01/24/16

The 545: Those Who Hold the Reins

1 President
9 Supreme Court Justices
100 Senators
435 Representatives

545 persons make decisions for 322,000,000+ persons and
      often affect the lives of millions more!

Many, most likely most, of these decision makers know little
      about the millions whose lives are affected by their choices.
The decision makers generally and genuinely listen to a
      handful of millionaires and billionaires.
Yet many of us everyday folks do not take the
      time/have the time to follow the deeds of this ever so
      small yet elite group of American citizens.
So many of us go about taking care of the basics and others of us the basics plus
      a bit more, expecting the 545 to make the Union at least approach
      perfect by establishing justice, insuring domestic tranquility, providing
      for the common defense, promoting the general welfare, and securing
      the blessings of liberty to ourselves and our posterity.

But how can they?
Too many often do as their slim minority of wealthy patrons bid.
Too many of them are preoccupied with getting and having it all for
      themselves and their loved ones instead of looking out for all of us
      who are heirs of this Constitution they are supposed to serve.

The reins ought to be in the hands of the people.
But finances have dislodged us people; the reins are not in our hands.

This is scary.
This is not working.
This is calling us to action.
For the first time in a long time, let's take the reins.

01/08/15

Past Time

A beloved house that squashed other wants because it
    came first
A beloved car that required sacrifice and scraping to
    obtain and maintain
Closets of clothes and shoes, many never worn
Beautiful linen evidently fit for a queen or someone of more
    importance than the owner because it was never used at her house
Kitchen appliances rarely and never used
Groceries long past expiration dates
Books, magazines, newspapers never read
Cds and dvds never heard, viewed
Seeds never planted, flower pots never filled
Bank accounts that will make someone happy, possibly the state
Remains of the remains
Remains that will be auctioned off to the highest bidder
    at much less than cost, remains often to
    be stashed the same way at another residence
All serve to remind some of us that life is fleeting and always fleeing.
Trust me: it's past time to get stepping, always past time.

08/19/15

Projection

Beware projection.
Others' projection on you and your projection on others.
More problems may be created than solved when projection is the rule.
Beware of assuming that someone will do in a situation what you would do in the situation.
Chances of predicting an individual's action are significantly different from predicting the action of a dog, especially an unfamiliar dog.
Significantly.

03/26/11

Laces

Football lovers know there's a time for laces out and there's a time for laces in.
What needs to be done determines which way to hold the ball.
Everyone knows the quarterback and the punter have different jobs.
Now if we could only apply this to life….

01/15/16

A Time Not to Ignore...

Montgomery bus boycott took 381 days before white Alabamians agreed that blacks did not have to sit in the back of the bus.

Do you know how long blacks had been telling officials blacks—colored—should not have to sit in the back of the bus?
Didn't you hear us?
We were ignored.

Mayor Rahm Emanuel invited a group of young black men to his office; following a brief discussion, Emanuel concluded young black men are treated differently by the police.
Do you know how long blacks have been telling officials all over the country this was true?
Didn't you hear us?
We were ignored.

Reports from many parts of the country reveal police officers framed African Americans.
Do you know how long blacks have been telling officials all over the country this was true?
Didn't you hear us?
We were ignored.

Please do not make me continue!

You have to hear us.
Note that "ignore" and "ignorant" are related.
The ends of both ignoring and ignorance are fast approaching.

If you persist, you ignore at your—and the country's—risk.
There's no time for each official to make a discovery.
Hear us; hear us now.
Get on the right side of history!
This is not a time to be ignorant nor ignore.

02/01/16

Funerals

Go to funerals.

The fewer persons expected to be there, the more important to go.

Go for the living.

The dead no longer—if they ever did—need us.

The living have so many needs!

If we can fill some of their needs by going to funerals, we should go.

Some attendees need to be told they did their best.

Some attendees need to be told that the dead loved them.

Some attendees need to be told the dead forgave them.

Some attendees need to be told the dead is in heaven.

Share anything you know that can help the bereaved.

But there's another reason to go to funerals.

Go for the stories!

All kinds of stories are told, most positive.

New facets of the individual are always revealed.

Doubtlessly you can learn something, perhaps help someone.

Go not only when you can squeeze one in.

Make time to go.

Go to funerals.

12/13/14

A Spring Chorus

The yard is singing.

Snow white candy tuft covers huge spots here and there.

Smaller and fewer spots of basket of gold sing as loudly.

Purple periwinkles line the sidewalk and the edge of the rockery.

A white one joins in now and then.

Lots and lots of bluebells pop up everywhere.

The evergreens seem greener.

The Easter lilies join the chorus.

The deck boxes spill over with more basket of gold, an array of
        tulips, pansies in just as many colors.

Enjoy today.

Recall in winter and fall.

04/11/15

Take Pictures!

Take pictures.
Really!
It's amazing what can be captured in a flash!
You can always throw away what you do not want.
But you can't capture that you did not catch.
Take pictures.
You can keep them forever!

The first day of baby's life or, alas, the last
The little kid in a cute Seahawk outfit, a senior decked out for a special
        occasion
A sibling reading to another sibling
A child astonished at the most "awesome" something.
A family/friend gathering
Graduations, weddings, anniversaries, vacations, achievements of any kind
Take pictures!
Date them; identify the subjects.
Enjoy!
Take pictures!

03/23/15

No, They Can't!

Everyone knows you can't make a silk purse out of a pig's ear or get
> blood from a turnip.

And yet, there are always folks who repeatedly attempt to make a silk
> purse out of a pig's ear or get blood from a turnip.

Some attempters know what they are trying to do, and they fight the odds.
Other attempters have no idea they are fighting an uphill and losing battle.
Someone should carefully explain to both groups no one can make a silk
> purse out of a pig's ear or get blood from a turnip.

06/29/15

DECLARATIONS

Life Lesson

Sometimes there is absolutely nothing I can do:
In instances where something needs to be done I hate not
      being able to do something.
All the talent, time, resources cannot change the results,
      could not have changed the results.
And the healthy person knows and accepts this truth.

03/23/15

Inside and Outside the Cave

There can be advantages to living in a cave:
      Familiarity
      Weather
      Space.

There can be disadvantages to living in a cave:
Same as the above.

12/08/14

Protection Nullified

When I was a little girl, I learned our government protects us.

When I was an older girl, I learned the government does not protect all of us equally.

When I was a teen-ager, I learned the government doesn't always protect us.

As a mature woman, I know for a fact that our government protects some people much more than it protects other people.

Today, despite what the government says, I know its ability to protect us is limited.
I hate to admit there are times the government can't protect us.
And worse, there are times when the government does not protect the most vulnerable among us.

09/11/01

What We Are

I used to quote often the fair but mentally ill Ophelia: "We know what we are but not what we may be."

I used to be awed by the irony that a mentally ill character could make such a statement, a statement I never doubted.

But now in addition to not knowing what we may be, I know at any given time we may not know what we are.

02/18/14

A Young Malawian Male and a Senior American Female Talk Dreams & Change

I can change.
I can change only myself.
I have knowledge to share.
I want to share my knowledge.
Everybody has knowledge.
But everyone does not wish to share.
The world I dream requires change.
But I cannot make others change.
I can only share my knowledge and hope they will listen.
Perhaps that is all any of us can do, share our knowledge and hope others will see.
But I fear the many who devalue human beings, who consider themselves
       superior to so many, if not everyone.
I fear they and their power will keep my dream of a better world only a dream.
But I will not abandon my dream.

Either the young man or the senior could have said every line.
Miles nor years altered what each wants.

01/20/16

A Picture

(On Looking at the Mug Shot of Rosa Parks)

A picture may be worth a thousand words.
Some pictures are worth more words; others fewer words.
Consider the mug shot of Rosa Parks, 7053.
The little lady who may look like a delicate hot house flower
        was in fact a steel magnolia.
Tired maybe, but far more tired of the discrimination than the
        day work that could be extremely tiring in many ways.
This little lady took on the South's power structure with the
        backing of the NAACP, of course, but she alone was on the
        bus, fingerprinted, in the jail cell....
No picture can show the toll of taking the bus everyday, never knowing whether
        she would be allowed on the bus, whether she would get a seat on the
        bus, or how long she could sit on the bus, or have to give up her seat on
        the bus.
The picture doesn't capture, can't capture how far she had come.
How many indignities did she suffer to collect less than minimum wage and no
        Social Security?
Did an employer or houseguest make a sexual overture or worse? How often?
How physically and mentally damaging was the overture?
How afraid was she?
Could she quit, change jobs, or have to return repeatedly to the
        same household?
How many times was there a replay?
How many times did she think there was danger when there
        was none—at this particular juncture?

Fight or flight exact the same toll although there may be no peril.
What's the weight, the cost of the stress?
And yet she paid, as so many paid, paid, and paid again.
Thank God we do not have to settle for a mug shot for her picture.
We can read her story and envision her quiet strength.

09/16/12

Irrelevancies

A friend died, passed, transitioned some say now.

I just saw him yesterday!
He was so young!
He was at rehearsal!
He was such a good person!
He has a beautiful family!
He was going to Hawaii!

We humans are amazing.
Whether we are God's favorite creation may be up for debate.
But we are amazing by any standard…
How recently we saw someone, age, activity, goodness,
       family, or plans do not take precedence.
The takeaway for me is to do what I want to do now, never
       aiming to hurt anyone, including myself.
One more time: there is no guarantee how long we'll be here.

12/23/13

Brain Dead

There are guidelines used to determine whether someone is brain dead:

Move the breathing tube.
Touch a cornea.
Tickle the throat.
Apply pressure.
Inflict pain.

However, there are persons who respond and thus pass all of these tests!
All the facts say their brains are not dead!

Yet, these not brain dead people take away food, shelter, clothing, education,
       and medical care from others expecting them to be, remain, or become
       sane.

We need another test for brain death.
Obviously the present tests are inadequate.

12/24/13

Excuses

Many well-meaning people attempt to make us do what we do not want to do….
I don't want any pie, cake, ice cream; I don't want anymore pie, cake, or ice
        cream, but the host urges, insists.
The same happens when I'm asked to take leftover food home.
The host urges, insists.
After so many no's, I agree—still not wanting the offerings.

To save time, I acquiesce.
Why doesn't the giver take no as my answer?
Why doesn't the receiver maintain no?

At some point it dawned on me that often in life people, usually well-meaning,
        shove something on me, at me, to me.
I say no, but they won't accept my no.
To save time or avoid hurting feelings, I eventually say yes.

I have to do better.
My no has to be no, more often.

12/16/15

The Folly of Agreeing to Disagree

There must be something we Americans agree on!

Not climate change
Not Keystone pipeline
Not Trans-Pacific Partnership, TPP
Not capital punishment
Not police action
Not health care
Not human rights
Not interracial marriage nor adoptions
Not gay marriage nor rights
Not foreign policy
Not universal pre-school
Not covering college costs
Not punishing bankers
Not immigration
Not foreign debt
Not using drones
Not being the number one arms provider
Not normalizing relations with Cuba
Not supporting Israel

Granted, some persons would argue they are not AGAINST some of
    these; their complaint is the COST of some of these.
They would argue that not having the money to finance any of the
    above makes agreeing to them unfeasible.
Only time will tell whether the pro or con was the right option.

COST, however, is the problem with selecting the wrong option, the
    COST to society for progress stymied, the cost to
    individuals for rights robbed.

12/09/14

The Ambivalence of Sharing

Sometimes I share and get certain responses.
And I think of the time I did share and the responses I got:
>Everyone knows that!
>Why did you tell that?
>Who wants to know?
>That's bragging!

So I decide to keep quiet.

Other times I share and get very different responses.

>I did not know that (and I need to know that)!
>I'm so glad you told me that!
>I'm going to tell Mom, Dad, Sis, Bro….
>I feel so much better for knowing this!
>I have a revelation I can use.
>I felt as if I were there!
>I'm going to do the same!

So I resolve to share.
And then there are times I refuse to share; the memory comes up but does not go out.

What I realize is a certain response is indeed just that: one response.
There may be others out there who neither want nor need just that piece of information and others who want that information to go no farther.

However, my dilemma remains: to share or not share.
Each situation comes with its rules.
I'll continue my way.

04/17/13

Worse Than Infidelity

"There are a lot of things worse than infidelity," said the veteran.
Ahh, thought the young woman: losing a limb or two or three is
        worse, a life-changing or shattering injury.
After a bit of thinking, she added
        living with a debilitating disease and/or its death sentence,
        losing a loved one,
        valuing a dollar more than a life,
        knowingly allowing an innocent person to suffer,
        persecuting a person for a congenital condition,
        originating, disseminating, and sustaining a lie.

Years of living, however, taught her that the
        hate, wrath of an "injured" party can also be worse than infidelity.
An injured party often makes a guilty party pay and pay and pay.
An injured party may say, "I forgive you," but never forgive.
Every action reminds the guilty party of his/her innocence and the other's guilt.
Yes, the veteran was right: "There are a lot of things worse than infidelity."

03/30/14

One-Sided Slights

She didn't cook the yams.
The family did not stop talking to the former spouse.
The loan was never repaid.
The inheritance was not equally divided.
An apology was never given.

Mind you, the injuring parties never knew about these injuries—or may have learned about them only years after the fact.
The injured revealed the injury to others but not the injuring one.

However, a relationship rift known by only one party can rob both "innocent" and "guilty" and be everlasting.

03/22/14

You Know That You Know

Have there been times when you knew you were right?
Any way the situation was viewed, you were right.
Yes, there was opposition.
You're not surprised.
But you knew; you knew if the opposition looked at the situation,
      voices would change, the opposition would become alliances.
So, despite the warning to proceed without the opposition, you paused,
      hesitated because you were so sure all you and they needed was time;
      time could make plain your stance; time could answer their questions.
So you waited and waited and waited.
By the time a similar situation arises, you see it, can summarize aptly.
Only after a very long wait do you finally realize that nothing you said nor
      the amount of time that passed moved the opposition.
As sad and disappointed as you feel, you continue the trudge, continue
      because you believe, continue because what you want for others
      matters much more than your feelings, disappointment.
There must be hope.

December, 2015

A Terrible Sadness

Of course, the pilot was ill.
Only an ill person would kill himself.
And to kill others, others who had nothing to do with his
       illness is more evidence of his illness.
The law of self-preservation is disregarded.
It was not in force for him that day.

So he always wanted to be a pilot.
Pardon me, but what if he had lived the kind of life that
       allowed space for other careers?
What if he had other interests and hobbies?

Grateful, most of us are not so focused on one area that
       we destroy ourselves and others if our dreams in that
       area are not fulfilled or thwarted.

04/06/15

Deceptive Looks

With a body like that, hair like that, please, is there anything you want?
Without taking a breath, she replied, "Funny you should say that. I was thinking about all the pain I feel now. I seem to attract accidents, had my fourth one four months ago, went pain-filled through twenties and thirties, now forties, feels I'll suffer the rest of my life."
Once again a reminder: (1) burdens, visible or invisible, seem
        to find all of us in one way or another (2) burdens are often
        unrecognized by anyone but the bearer.

04/11/15

Every Student Can Learn

Every student can learn.

A simple statement.

Simple as in elementary, rudimentary.

Simple as in dumb some would say.

Simple not as question or exclamation.

Simple as declaration.

Simple as in breathing, eating, growing, reproducing, responding to stimuli.

ANYONE who needs to be given this information should not be teaching a student about whom this information must be given.

Repeat: ANYONE who needs to be given this information should not be teaching a student about whom this information must be given.

Why?

Because this teacher has the preconceived notion that this child can't learn.

A child cannot overcome this teacher's prejudice.

The teacher's prejudice takes precedence over the child's learning.

Every society needs teachers who have never wondered if every child can learn, teachers who intuitively know every child can learn and have always gone about teaching students accordingly.

02/01/16

Doing and Being

"Just stop. Do what the policeman says."
She meant well.
She believed she had the answer.
ALL the stopped individual had to do was obey!
She was trying to save somebody.
And this is a black woman!

What she did not see, get, understand was this:
> A black male of any age often does not have to DO anything,
> He may not be DOING anything.
> So often his crime is BEING.

The crime is being!
No list contains the many times blacks, browns, "others"—men and
> women—have been stopped by police.
Often nothing says why—the real why—they were stopped.
Too, too many times, times we'll never know, black men—and women—
> are stopped, arrested, sentenced, killed for being black.
Look how many times some persons are shot.
One, two, three bullets may have rendered them dead.
But no, sixteen, twenty-eight, …
To the killer, scum—not someone's son or daughter—is dead, over dead.

PLEASE UNDERSTAND.
And this nation so great at giving us figures has no figures for the number
> killed by those deemed protectors.
Perhaps numbers would make believers of some folks.
Perhaps not.
Some of us can only do and be.
A student, star athlete, professor—any can be killed,
> not because of doing but all because of being.

02/05/15

Crumbling

There are at least 100 ways to crumble.

Retreat.

Shrivel.

Explode.

Implode.

Bang.

Whimper.

        ABOVE ARE SOME OF THE WAYS TO CRUMBLE.

The problem: We rarely get to choose how we crumble.

We just do.

Before and after another's crumbling, we who manage to survive have
        to protect ourselves as best we can.

But because we do not, cannot always protect ourselves, we cannot, do
        not always avoid someone else's crumbling.

Besides, we ourselves may be in an as yet unidentified crumbling mode.

04/03/14

Present: After 50 Years

Voter Registration Instructor
Freedom Rider follower
Set to go to The March

Told can't sit in front of bus
Sisters arrested at white library
Court guards making whites sit on white side, coloreds sit on colored side

Set to go to The March
Then Mom said, "No, you can't go."
No discussion, revisiting, negotiating
"You can't go."
Girl/woman did not go.

Years later, long after Mom departed, I now understand why mothers
    sometimes say no.
Now I understand why Birmingham Mothers said their daughters
    could not go, sent them to Sunday School instead.
Now I understand why the Fruitvale Mother told her son not to
    drive but take BART instead.

All the odds said moms were right.
But….
I understand good Mothers want to protect children, although
    Mothers' decisions may disappoint, even anger children.
I believe the children know August 24th and again August 28th I
    was there for them and thousands more.
And I think Mother would have consented.

10/24/13

Post-Traumatic-Stress Syndrome

Maybe all of us have post-traumatic-stress syndrome.
All of us certainly have battles.
Circumstances call us out or drag us in.
Some of us travel the globe.
Others stay home.
Some battle the one or the many, known and unknown, good and bad.
A large number battle self.
The war rages, sometimes visibly, other times invisibly
      sometimes outwardly, other times inwardly.
Hot war, cold war; abuse from a thousand origins; discrimination on
      countless levels; burdens from family, friends, and foes; illness marked
      curable or not; jobs physical, mental, menial—ranking near worthless.
For the trauma—that we can or cannot reveal, will or will not reveal—looms
      with and over the traumatized.
No advice dissipates it.
Managing to cope is a devoutly wished desire, if we are sane enough to
      have such a wish.
But, once again, wishing does not make it so.
Now, if only the stress following the disorder would pass as
      did the incident that precipitated the stress.

11/18/14

Responses

Some days we smile.
Some days we actually laugh.
Some days we cry.
Some days we are so angry, we simply….
On second thought, we do nothing simply, scarcely ever have that
    opportunity.
Sometimes on rare, very rare occasions, we fight back rather than take a
    deep breath and swallow, never guessing our responses will require
    more responses.
Sometimes we are surprised the others' responses are about their perceptions
    of us rather than our responses.
By the time the others have gotten their words in—and they will get them
    in—we are often beginning to wish we had gulped more air and
    remained silent.
But wide awake, we continue to dream of a day when we can be who we
    are and what we are without someone taking offense, patronizing,
    or chastising.
We look forward to and work for the day when there will be no need to
    defend our name.
We know that day is coming.

We do not apologize for being tired nor anxious as we do whatever is in
    our power to make that day come sooner rather than later.

01/24/14

A Warning

No prophet, seer, or clairvoyant
Just a speaker who has dealt with a lot of people in many situations often over a three-month period.
Everything I know says the behavior of some Americans is increasingly negative.
This, I say, is not a fluke.
Not being a conspiracy advocate, I do not want to say this was planned.
But our country has not cashed the promissory note given many.
As long as there were signs—though often misread—that time and hard work would solve the problems, most trudged on.
But now, with unemployment and underemployment, low wages and high costs, more people see the gap between what they need/want and what they have/attain widening.
Consequently, they are often prompted to do what they never before would have considered.
So, some families break down; some parents and children ignore or abandon their responsibilities, kill families, classmates, teachers; some kill co-workers; some kill randomly; some kill themselves.
Many, through little or no fault of their own, are at risk.

If government and the private sector cannot, do not, or will not provide employment so that persons can get the food, clothing, shelter, health care, and education needed, society will continue this downward spiral.
And increasingly we will see what happens when dreams are deferred and the center does not hold.

11/02/13

Carrying the Ball

"The Sixties people dropped the ball!
They let us down, left us hanging!"

It took everything to cover what could have
    been a "Go, Hawks" scream.
How could she say that?
Not wanting to hurt or condemn, I sat fuming
    as the conversation moved to other topics.
The comment made me answer how we did
    not drop the ball, how we carried the burden and
    carry the burden today, how scars cover our
    bodies mentally and spiritually and sometimes physically.
We went to all of those white high schools
    and colleges where so many people did
    not want us to go. We usually skip reunions.
The fun part of these educational institutions
    never materialized for us: we spent most
    of our time alone or in a corner with the
    one or two other black students; people
    shut doors in our faces; they bumped into
    us; they knocked books out of our hands.
    Teachers were rarely helpful. If the
    principal was involved, we were almost
    always the ones suspended or expelled.
Many of us had to go to another school or university;
    some of us never completed formal school.
On the rare occasions when a white student
    asked us for help with an assignment, that student
    got a B, and we got a D.

We were told we should be in another department.
We were convinced to change our majors.
We were encouraged to take sabbaticals—all
    we had to do was write the dissertation.
Upon attempting to re-enter, some of us in the programs were told we
    did not meet the requirements. One man reluctantly took a sabbatical at his advisors' suggestion—allow others to participate in this small program, advisors said. When he attempted to re-enter, he was told his 3.8 grade point was too low. The program required a 3.5. "We have so many applicants with 4.0 that we are not looking at anything but 4.0 grade points."
After years of attempting to get terminal degrees, we received letters, letters
    telling us the school had made an error, we should not have been admitted to the program.
Some of us left one university and went to another where we discovered what
    we had left.
Some of us went to other countries; one friend went to Scotland, got his Ph.D.
    too—and minus the hassling!
We endured parents who said, "Leave those white people alone. When the
    Lord is ready for you to go in those places, He'll make a way."
And some of us went to jobs where we found ourselves in the same situation.
Despite how good we were, we were always "affirmative action" employees and
    definitely not qualified. We were the token one or one of two or three. We trained persons who were younger, less educated, less experienced, and less skilled. These trainees were often promoted to jobs we never got.
Because of our single-mindedness, some of us are/were poor spouses and poor
    parents. Because of our preoccupation, we divorced or were divorced, some of us more than once.

Some of us are mentally and spiritually and often physically scarred.
Half a century later we continue to ask ourselves did we do what needed to be done. We want to know if we had taken another route if all would be better now. We can't stop thinking about that time.
Whether we did or did not get the degrees, we paid a high price, younger sister. Those of us still here are still paying. Drugs, alcohol, prison, suicide took some of us. So much of what you can do today is the result of standing on our shoulders, shoulders that are often invisible to you.
How different would life be if we had chosen to sit through the Sixties?
There are more examples. These were the first to come to mind.
All of a sudden I thought about how long I was upset with Roy Wilkins.
> I kept telling myself that he should have known better. He was an adult; we were kids. What did we know?

Then one day as clearly as could be I realized that Roy Wilkins was not guilty. He was almost as innocent as we were. Roy Wilkins had no way of knowing just how much of a battle integration would be. He could never have imagined that some human beings would treat other human beings in such a sub-human fashion. Perhaps he had not thought legislatures can never legislate what transpires in hearts and minds.

> I immediately forgave him, wish I could have thanked him.

So, I realize the young lady did to us Sixties folks what I did to Mr. Wilkins.
Perhaps one day she will see as I see.
How many times do we have to take the same hills?
The only answer: as many times as we have to take the same hills.
Some hills can't be given to the enemy.

Dear younger brothers and sisters, though we lost thousands, maybe
> millions with the assassinations of Dr. Martin Luther King, Jr., and
> Senator Robert F. Kennedy, the great majority of us are still here, still
> fighting.

Many of us continue working never having gotten the justice at the end
> of that arc. We take care of children and grandchildren, neighbor
> children, go to school meetings, teach—often without pay.

Despite being in our sixties, seventies, eighties, and even nineties, many of us
> continue to carry the ball, we have never dropped it.

We did not leave you hanging; we did not let you down.

We never would.

11/7/14
Revised
11/6/15

My Undone List

Frame cards of pairs of birds

Sort photographs

Compose collages

Organize scrapbooks

Check definitions, "stellar jay" and "murder of crows," for example

Read more of those Great Books and listen to Great Courses

Check out all of those biographies and autobiographies

View films, especially those Oscar-nominated ones

Take some Great Courses

Write more poems/stories/plays/essays

Finish all the poems I began and stories I think about

Review all of the notes for poems, stories, essays

Take tours

See sights

Clean closets and drawers

Teach and take classes

Volunteer more

Contact long lost family, friends, students

Memorize song lyrics

Clean my bedroom

Meet a few well-known folks to have great conversations

In short, haha, I want to visit the caves I exited too quickly or missed entirely!

April, May, 2015

High School Reunions

Of course, we couldn't know how this Class would turn out!

Of course!

Of course.

School

Marriage

Children

Divorces

Grandchildren

Deaths of parents, siblings, administrators, teachers, children,
       grandchildren, heroes

No one could have guessed who would die so young.

Oh, someone could have speculated, but no one could know.

War—sorry, police action for Vietnam

Diseases of every kind, including drugs and alcohol

Jobs, careers we love

Jobs, careers we hate

The way we were, what we were

What we are, the way we are

Happy everyone's here

Sad for all of those absent, especially the living

But always wise enough to know we are blessed—**REGARDLESS.**

12/13/14

A Man Worth Admiring

Worked hard all of his life
Worked for God, family, church, community, and country
Worked for anyone anywhere all of the time, often no pay
Worked as defender, protector, provider
Worked so that many folks in many places could have a better life

Admitted he had a good life
Acknowledged God as source of his strength

Opportunities provided by retirement presented more time to help
        more people more often
Onward as much if not more than ever before
Overrun by ill health eventually
Outside his home was a better place
Overburdened wife and he agreed.

One year, two years, three years, four
"Ordered steps led here?" asked he who always asked that his steps
        be ordered.
Outlawed questions to God
Objected never to his interpretation of God's will

Outlook dimmed
Overtaken by Orthodox questions
Over time gradually, intentionally shut down

Clear eyes said he recognized visitors.
Could visitors have been wrong?

Could not talk, said some.
Can so talk, vowed others.
Conversed when he wanted to some folks believed.
All saw his anger.

Missed message apparent:
Missions that accomplished good deeds—and perhaps, bad deeds—
    are irrelevant, not withstanding.
The ease with which we move nor the method or mode of the move
    toward vacating these premises is not guaranteed.
Only the move is definite.

11/19/14

The Ignorant Prodigal

How could the Prodigal Son have known he didn't know?
How was he to know he couldn't keep his word?
He meant what he said when he said it.
But things happened, not without cause but in the midst of causes,
    many causes over which he had little or no control.
He showed his face, but the world saw a mask, a mask they misread
    and misunderstood, a face mask they did not want to know.
The bubbles he made existed but not for long.
Being next to a hammer of any kind increases the possibility of
    bubbles being destroyed.
So much is not in his hand, despite its being large and long.
Never mind his intention and preparation.
The hand can't, doesn't, won't handle everything he faces.
He can work on putting his ear to the ground, and he may get closer
    to his goal.
But variables assure there is no way he can ever know what he
    needs to clarify the known and conquer the unknown.
He does not know what he does not know.

11/06/04   Inspired by Scott Mansfield painting *Unbeknownst*

If You Lived Here...

All may look fine—nice house on a clean street, Daddy manicuring the yard,
    Mom carrying in the groceries, children playing in the yard.
To an outsider who has enough information to know all is not well, to know
    the house is on fire, naturally comes the question why not vacate the
    premises.
Reasons are legion.
There are as many reasons as there are trapped people, plus a few more.
I am loyal.
I made a vow.
I want the status.
I have too much invested; it's cheaper to keep her/him.
I don't want to lower my standard of living.
I don't want to hurt anyone.
I don't want to be alone; I may not find anyone.
I could do worse.
I fear what they will say.
I fear what they would think.
The kids need me.
The spouse needs me.
The spouse is a good person.

My religion forbids it.

Sadly, the house won't stop burning if the parties remain the same.
Eventually the inhabitants feel not just the heat.
The fire catches them!
And never is it confined to the two of them and their offspring.

There's smoke damage, sometimes asphyxiation.
The flames singe, sometimes mortally wounding—those inside as
    well as those outside.
However, just as the flames did not spontaneously begin, they will not
    spontaneously end.

So, beware of things and people wearing flames.
Whether inside or outside, you could get burned.
Worse, you can get burned inside AND outside!

10/1505   Inspired by Jessica Dodge's painting *If You Lived Here*

What You're Getting Into

Baby screams, twists and turns,
Has no idea what it's getting into.

Possible Scenarios
Mom and Dad love it.
Mom loves it.
Dad loves it.
A family member loves it.
A stranger loves it.

Any of the above could resent or hate baby just as easily—or more easily!
Masquerading as parents, foster parents, or caregivers, haters, abusers, and
       misusers are often in here and out there.
More than we know or want to know, they walk—creep, crawl, or
       slink—among us.

The five-year old who sipped from stepmom's grape soda
The angel-looking child whose parents saw only demons
The child who wet the bed
The child who refused to eat the food
The child who was refused food

Children know not what they are getting into when
       they get into something.

And semen and egg donors often do not know what they are
       getting into when they get into combining egg and sperm, be it
       planned or unplanned.

02/22/14

Relativity

I can't stand this kind of soup; he would love to have any soup.
I'm tired of walking; she wishes she could walk.
I hate icing my arm; she wishes she had an arm.
I'm not to swim for three to four months; he never learned to swim.

"Relative" is the word.

02/19/14

The Message

Regardless of the message, everybody never gets it.
Everybody does not see it, hear it.
Ones who hear do not always believe it.
Others do not take it seriously.
Some do not understand it.
Some misunderstand it.
All of the above notwithstanding, the message is the same.

12/26/15

MUSINGS

Plusses & Minuses

When Gimbel's Department store opened in 1887 with its many entrances,
      everybody saw the plus—access, access, access!
When the store closed in 1986, it had the highest rate of shoplifting in the world!
The doors that were a plus became a minus.
Such is life: The day may come when plusses become minuses.

01/23/16

What Is Sanity?

"I have to keep searching for my family; that is the only way to keep my sanity,"
      said a Japanese looking for his family killed in the tsunami.

What some people say is that his sanity is gone; that he manages to continue out
      of sheer determination is insanity.
He continues his work; no one interrupts.
If he stopped, he might regain his sanity and go insane.

04/16/14

Questions That Don't Need to Be Asked

Why is your hair so short?
Why are your lips so big?
Why are your legs so skinny?
Why are you so fat?
Why are you so dark?
Why is your skin like that?

12/13/14

What Folks Miss

"I never got into reading," said my decades-old Christian friend.
"I don't read fiction," said my PhD friend.
"I read only the Bible," said my twenty-nine–year-old student.
I think about what they've missed.
And then I wonder in all of my reading what I've missed.

11/11/14

That Shakespeare Mind

When Shakespeare was writing his version of *Hamlet*, he could
> not possibly have known he was giving the world such a masterpiece,
> that he was giving posterity words, phrases, lines
> that would become staples of the language,
> that concepts in the play so often explain the mind—the pettiness and
> the loftiness—of humans worldwide throughout history.

There are Hamlets all over the world deciding whether to
> be or not to be and in between dispensing advice worth
> listening to; they're a small minority.

There are Gertrudes believing having a man, even if
> he's her brother-in-law, is the number one—maybe only—
> reason to live.

There are Poloniuses whose lives pivot on what they call helping
> when in actuality they do as much if not more harm than
> good.

There are Ophelias who between what they bring upon
> themselves and what is thrust upon them lack the mental
> strength to bear the weight.

There are Laerteses whose impulsiveness regularly harms
> others and themselves.

There are Claudiuses who overcome any barrier to achieve
> their goals despite the cost.

There are Ghosts who are not real yet take up residence in our
> minds, all but stop our lives filling our heads with commentary.

There are Horatios who are willing sounding boards and
> summarizers.

There are buddies Rosencrantz & Guildenstern, two peas in a
 pod, who miss the big picture as they unwittingly play the
 role of pawn, often to their detriment.
There are the Fortinbrases who always seem to know the exact
 time to move or stay, stand or sit.

The world should be forever grateful to Shakespeare.

After seeing *Hamlet* one more time									*11/14/14*

Wondering and Knowing

Did you ever wonder why in the world you made a particular decision?
Did you ever wonder what in the world were you thinking?

You know:
marriage began/ended;
child conceived/not conceived;
property bought/sold;
letter mailed/ not mailed;
position accepted/rejected;
check signed/unsigned;
class completed/discontinued.

Did you know the choice was wrong the next minute, hour, day,
        week, month, or year?
Or did it take years, a decade, a lifetime to realize the error?
Did you come to see that the choice changed your life profoundly?

I just wonder.
Somehow it seems one act in an instant ought not divide our
        lives into before and after.
It seems.
And yet I know one act can indeed divide our lives.

I know there are times when absolutely nothing can remove,
        erase, or delete the act.
We cannot go back to before the act despite the many times we or others say
        if only....
I know.
About this fact I do not wonder.

11/13/14

My Mom's Letters

I wish I had known to keep many, if not all, of
>   my mother's letters when I was a freshman
>   in college.

I received two letters each day—one in the morning
>   mail and one in the afternoon mail.

I did not write her everyday, but as soon as I
>   responded, I put her letters in the trash.

A maid at work, M'Dear did not always have
>   paper, so she would write on the gas bill or
>   the light bill, a brown paper bag.

One year she did not have a card for my December birthday, so she took a
>   Christmas card, drew lines through "Merry" and "Christmas," and
>   wrote "Happy Birthday."

I do have the memories—and the memories are usually quite
>   satisfying; still I wish I had kept the letters, probably always will.

She kept my letters, all letters, but a well-meaning sister
>   destroyed them before other siblings arrived for M'Dear's funeral, said
>   she did not want us fussing.

I have one letter I had not answered and another that was in the
>   mail when she died.

Nobody has to tell me to keep them.

2:42 a. m. by the light of the Mac
under a mosquito net in Malawi   *01/24/16*

What to Keep

I regret not knowing early in life what to keep.
There ought to be a guide.
I'm not talking about official papers: birth
      certificates, wedding licenses, diplomas, warranties, tax forms, etc.

I'm talking about church programs and school programs, awards.
I wish I had known, for instance, to keep many, if not all, of
      my mother's letters when I was a freshman
      in college.
With cell phones and You Tube, we can have unlimited records of
      this kind.
Now all we need is something or someone to tell us what to keep.

01/24/16

Christian: The Lion

The first time I saw the video of the reunion of Christian the Lion and two
    young men who loved him, I cried.
Yes, a lion in Africa and two men in England I'd never know made
    me cry.
Christian was so happy to see the young men Rendall and Bourke.
On his hind legs, he turned from one to the other and back again,
    always giving lion hugs, huge lion hugs.
A viewer could tell Christian could not tell whom to hug how long.
He went back and forth and back and forth between the young men.
Then Christian brought his wife to meet his human friends!
Nobody was in any danger; the men would not kill the lion; Christian and
    his wife would not eat the men.
Christian was very young when the men got him.
They romped with him.
They kept him until he got too big to live with them.
Sadly, they took him home, to his home, the jungle of Africa.
They went to visit him after one year.
The video records this reconciliation.

I waited to hear the video was staged.
After more than a decade, no such word.
I think about Christian, how he must have felt being alone, what
    adjusting to the alien environment must have been.
I am certain he missed/misses the young men.
I wonder how often he thought/thinks about them.
He must have felt, must feel abandoned.
I wonder if he thought he had done wrong, that they no longer
    cared for him.

I know Christian doesn't understand that he had to stay in the
	jungle, that the men can't stay in the jungle.
He's just a lion.

And then I think about the many abandoned children and what they
	must think.

01/24/16

Duped

Duped—by strange white men and fellow black men
Duped again over 200 years later with the Emancipation
        Proclamation
Duped yet again with Reconstruction
Duped with the 40 acres and a mule
Duped with separate but equal
Duped with integration

What happened to fool me once?
Fool me twice?

Haven't we been duped sufficiently?
Does no one remember/realize/know that we have indeed
        been duped?

No more duping.
No more duping!

The duped will no longer be duped.
A powder keg nears its explosive point.
The cost to attackers and liars will exceed the present-day cost
        to the downtrodden.
A new norm will be instituted.
Prepare for a rumble this time, a rumble like no other.
The duped are determined to be deceived no longer.
The duped will speak and spread the truth.

02/11/14

Unmarried

Years spent trying to be what she was not
        because he was not what she thought he was,
She realized she was not what he thought she was.
Each wanted the other to be something neither was.
No malice on either's part, simply ignorant of what was.

Wisely not wanting to shape a mate nor become what the
        mate wanted, she reasoned not married could not be as
        uncomfortable as unmarried.
He protested.
She knew better.
Not an up nor an out existed for the two.
Hating being part of the statistics but hating suffocating
        more, she filed.
He and most of those who did not agree came to see
        the divorce has made all the difference in both their lives.

02/11/14

Starting Again

A free ride to a bus station, bus ticket in hand
Less than minimum-wage savings in my pocket
Dressed in prison khakis
Armed only with a skill that may be useless,
I leave my real world where few decisions were required.
I followed the rules and got to leave earlier.
I could have disobeyed and suffered the
      consequences, consequences ranging from solitary
      confinement to bodily harm, death maybe.
But I chose to manage.
I managed better and longer than I could ever have imagined.
My debt to society paid, I now go to the much larger
      and more complex real world.
I walk out with no support.
With few services in sight and the limited wraparound
      services unavailable, I take responsibility for myself.
My life will forever be divided into Before Prison and After Prison.
But today, with my past in place and lessons learned, I begin anew.

01/30/14

In the Same Situation

Standing up for myself says I am bold to some and foolish
    to others.
Walking away says I am brave to some and afraid to others.
Remaining in a situation says I am strong to some and
    weak to others.
Forgiving someone says I am sensible to some and
    senseless to others.
Try as I might, I can think of nothing that has one vantage
    point only.
Though a dilemma may appear to be the case, experience
    tells me rare are the situations in which there are two
    choices only.
There are often countless points between one extreme and the other.
So, despite the supporters and opponents, I am the one who
    must decide.
Sometimes I can and will explain; other times I won't or
    can't explain.
This I know: the serenity that comes after the choice is my
    only evidence of having chosen correctly—for now.

10/04/12

What Would You Do?

If you had to capture persons to be taken from their country to
    another country to be slaves, would you?
If you had to gas or intern persons because of their ethnicity,
    would you?
If you had to drop bombs on a city, would you?
If you saw boats of people from another country coming to
    your country, would you turn them back?

In each instance the hoped for answer is no.
In each instance experience shows there are
    those persons who would not hesitate to say yes.
This truth shows how human beings do indeed repeat history,
    that results of earlier choices regularly fail to influence
    many of us to choose the opposite, that too many persons never
    imagine themselves in a similar position wanting others to choose
    differently.

12/08/15

The Sound of Children

Squeal!
Another squeal, a bit shriller.
A raucous laugh.
A belly laugh.
A yell.
Another scream.
That's the sound of children playing, having fun.
I've heard them on Lake Malawi.
I've heard them on Lake Washington.
I've seen them on the Atlantic and Pacific coasts.
I've splashed with them in the Indian Ocean.
In every instance there were squeals, laughter, screams and more
    of the same.
The children were always under ten.
I did not always know what they were saying, but I always
    knew they were having fun.
And I wish they could continue to have fun.
I wish they could give this fun to folks older than ten all over the world.
I wish.

02/01/16

The Cracked Window

The cracked window for good things black is closing.
The young American-African president born in the USA
      opened the window wider than ever before.
But the opening is still a mere crack.
The young president could not, did not
      open the window wide; he did the best he could: he
      increased the size of the crack.
His and the hard work of many others cracked this window
      but only for a short time.
Eight years cannot possibly repair, rectify the centuries of lost,
      stolen history, rectify the murderous behavior.
Almost any attempt to do good was met with powerful opposition
      as the rich got richer and grabbed more and the poor got poorer
      and lost more.
Many tried and still try their best to close the window, keep
      closed.
And the size of the crack decreases in less than a year unless we work
      extremely hard to keep it open.
Through this cracked window came light that afforded many
      a sight they had never before seen.
Their exposure to black life was real and broad.
No longer did they see only the millionaire stars,
      "personalities," and athletes, that infinitesimal group
      many—from the man on the street to Supreme Court
      justices—choose to use as proof affirmative action is no
      longer necessary.

For the first time, many saw the conflict between the masses,
> the everyday people and police, could understand the
> negative attitudes of so many blacks, browns all over
> the land.

Fearing for their lives, police officers mowed down citizens
> as young as twelve and as old as ninety-three, the innocent and the ill.

Rarely was one bullet adequate to stop a black person,
> always guilty 'til proven innocent.

Rarely was a policeman indicted; forget the word "convicted"
> though occasionally the aggrieved collected taxpayer money.

For the first time, others saw what many blacks had seen
> for centuries.

For the first time a record of the number of citizens killed by police
> is being kept though all police are not always using the same standard.

A centuries'-old cry should be resurrected: No taxation
> without representation.

"Occupy" became the call word.
No New Jim Crow became a mantra.
Black Lives Matter, no too or also necessary.
Demonstrate constantly that this is the case.
Many of every color profess and protest constantly.

So show whatever needs to be shown through the window
> these last few months.

Get more poems, novels, and plays in any form you choose.
Get more slave narratives published and filmed, more
> Butlers, 42s, Fruitvales, and Comptons.

Get more songs, paintings, music, and dance.
Get more Coateses and Pittses, more Herberts in print.

Get more news stories of the horrors, inconsistences, unfairness.
Get more voters registered, of course!
But get more registered voters to vote!
Get more winning, honest, responsible candidates.
Speak truth; speak truth in your way.
Give details.
Know that Joy DeGruy named "the problem" Post-Traumatic-
       Slave Syndrome in 2005, when the crack was much smaller.
Know that blacks are not the only ones afflicted with the
       dis-ease.
This dis-ease eats all of us, some at a much faster, more ravishing
       pace than others.
Know that enclosing persons—yes, persons, human beings—
       in cages rather than houses, good jails rather than good
       schools makes folks act less than human and not
       the God-created beings they are.

Remember: only the size of the crack is a bit larger.
We can do our best to keep the crack open by learning
       from the exposure.
Or we can suffer more negative consequences of the crack's
       narrowing, if not disappearing.
We need that light.
We—all of us—can do the uncomfortable and the inconvenient to put
       out the fires engendered by this closing of the crack; we
       can make the crack sufficiently wider soon.
OR WE CAN HAVE OUR HANDS FILLED WITH
       BATTLING THE FIRE NEXT TIME.

01/20/16

INDEX

An Act	27
Adam and Eve and That Fruit	33
The Ambivalence of Sharing	72
Arguments Against the Death Penalty	5
Brain Dead	68
Carrying the Ball	85
Christian: the Lion	108
The Cracked Window	116
Crumbling	80
Culture	19
Dali Clocks	43
Deceptive Looks	77
Declarations	
Doing and Being	79
Don't Call Me Mother!	38
Duped	110
Every Student Can Learn	78
Exclamations	
Excuses	69
The 545: Those Who Hold the Reins	48
Folly of Agreeing to Disagree	70
Fragility	8
Funerals	54

The Greens	40
Halloween Horror	11
High School Reunions	90
If You Lived Here	94
The Ignorant Prodigal	93
Images of Crying Women	25
Imperatives	
Inside and Outside the Cave	61
Interrogatives	
In the Same Situations	113
The Interview	24
Irrelevancies	67
I Thought Wrong	34
Journals Never Written	47
The Laces	51
Life Lesson	61
List Goes On	10
Living in the Present	29
A Man Worth Admiring	91
The Message	97
Muscle and Might	6
Musings	
My Mom's Letters	106

My Undone List	89
No Boundaries	15
No, They Can't!	57
One-Sided Slights	74
Past Time	50
A Picture	65
Plusses and Minuses	101
Post-Traumatic-Stress Syndrome	82
Present: After 50 Years	81
The Problem with the Minimum	36
Projection	51
Protection Nullified	62
Questions	3
Questions That Don't Need to Be Asked	102
The Real Spectrum	37
Relativity	97
Responses	83
Sanctioned Murder	13
The Simple Things	23
The Sound of Children	115
A Spring Chorus	55
Starting Again	112
Surprised Again	30

Take Pictures!	56
A Terrible Sadness	76
That Don't Make No Sense	22
That Shakespeare Mind	103
This Is Going On	20
A Time Not to Ignore	52
Titanic Errors	14
To the Lady Who Wanted to Know	9
Two Lovely Couples	41
Unmarried	111
A Warning	84
What Is God Doing?	2
What Is Sanity?	101
What to Keep	107
What We Are	63
What Would You Do?	114
What You're Getting Into	96
Where Is God?	1
Who's Lying	28
Wondering and Knowing	105
Worse Than Infidelity	73
You Know That You Know	75
A Young Malawian	64
Youth or the Sea	31

About the Author

GEORGIA STEWART MCDADE, a Louisiana native who has lived in Seattle more than half her life, loves reading and writing. Earning a Bachelor of Arts from Southern University, Master of Arts from Atlanta University, and Ph. D. from University of Washington, the English major spent more than thirty years teaching at Tacoma Community College but also found time to teach at Seattle Community College, Seattle University, the University of Washington, Lakeside School, Renton Technical College, and Zion Preparatory Academy. As a charter member of the African-American Writers' Alliance (AAWA), McDade began reading her stories in public in 1991. For a number of years she has written poems inspired by art at such sites as Gallery 110, Seattle Art Museum, Columbia City Gallery, and Onyx Fine Arts Collective. For several years she wrote for Pacific Newspapers, especially the *South District Journal*. The prolific writer has edited several books and has works in AAWA anthologies *I Wonder as I Wander, Gifted Voices, Words? Words! Words*, and *Threads*. Her books include *Travel Tips for Dream Trips* (1988), questions and answers about her six-month, solo trip around the world; *Outside the Cave* (2009), *Outside the Cave II* (2012), and *Outside the Cave III* (2016), collections of poetry; *Observations and Revelations* (2016), a collection of stories, sketches, and essays; and numerous other poems, stories, and essays. Among her several writing projects are the journals kept during her travels, two biographies, and an examination of the novels of Jessie Fauset.

www.ingramcontent.com/pod-product-compliance
Lightning Source LLC
Chambersburg PA
CBHW052308300426
44110CB00035B/2177